Masters of Music

THE WORLD'S GREATEST COMPOSERS

The Life and Times of

Franz Joseph Haydn

Mitchell Lane
PUBLISHERS

P.O. Box 619
Bear, Delaware 19701

Masters of Music

THE WORLD'S GREATEST COMPOSERS

Titles in the Series

The Life and Times of...

Visit us on the web: www.mitchelllane.com
Comments? email us: mitchelllane@mitchelllane.com

Masters of Music

THE WORLD'S GREATEST COMPOSERS

The Life and Times of

Franz Joseph Haydn

by Susan Zannos

Printing   1   2   3   4   5   6   7   8
Library of Congress Cataloging-in-Publication Data
Zannos, Susan.
        Franz Joseph Haydn/Susan Zannos.
                p. cm. — (Masters of Music. The world's greatest composers)
        Summary: Discusses the life and career of the eighteenth century Austrian composer.
        Includes bibliographical references (p.) and index.
                ISBN 1-58415-193-5
                1. Haydn, Joseph, 1732-1809—Juvenile literature. 2. Composers—Austria—Biogra-
        phy—Juvenile literature. [1. Haydn, Joseph, 1732-1809. 2. Composers.] I Title. II. Series.
        ML3930.H3 Z36 2003
        780'.92—dc21

                                                                        2002153348

ABOUT THE AUTHOR: Susan Zannos has been a lifelong educator, having taught at all levels, from preschool to college, in Mexico, Greece, Italy, Russia, and Lithuania, as well as in the United States. She has published a mystery *Trust the Liar* (Walker and Co.) and *Human Types: Essence and the Enneagram* (Samuel Weiser). Her book, *Human Types*, was recently translated into Russian, and in 2003 Susan was invited to tour Russia and lecture about her book. Another book she wrote for young adults, *Careers in Education* (Mitchell Lane) was selected for the New York Public Library's "Books for the Teen Age 2003 List." She has written many books for children, including *Chester Carlson and the Development of Xerography* and *The Life and Times of Ludwig van Beethoven* (Mitchell Lane). Her great interest in classical composers inspired her to write this book. When not traveling, Susan lives in the Sierra Foothills of Northern California.

PHOTO CREDITS: Cover: Photo Researchers; p. 6 Photo Researchers; p. 9 Corbis; p. 10 Archivo Iconografico; p. 12 Austrian Archives/Corbis; p. 14 Hulton/Archive; p. 17 Austrian Archives/Corbis; p. 18 Stephanie Kondrchek; p. 19 Ali Meyer/Corbis; p. 22 Archivo Iconografico/Corbis; p. 25 left and right: Corbis; p. 28 Corbis; p. 34 Photo Researchers; p. 37 Hulton/Archive; p. 38 SuperStock; p. 40 Bettmann/Corbis; p. 42 Bettmann/Corbis.

PUBLISHER'S NOTE: This story is based on the author's extensive research, which she believes to be accurate. Documentation of this research can be found on page 46.

Sometimes, the spelling of names can differ through translation and you will find many variations in other published works. We have chosen the more Anglicized spelling of some names, such as Joseph (instead of Josef) and Nikolaus (instead of Miklós).

The internet sites referenced in this book were all active as of the publication date of this book. Because of the fleeting nature of some Web sites, the publisher cannot guarantee that they will all be active when you are reading this book.

Contents

The Life and Times of

Franz Joseph Haydn

by Susan Zannos

Franz Joseph Haydn has been called the father of the symphony. However, Haydn did not write the first symphony. He developed it from a short, simple form to a long form for a large orchestra. The combination of instruments that he used in his symphonies are the basis for today's symphony orchestra. This portrait of Haydn was done by Ludwig von Guttenbrunn.

Papa Haydn

F ranz Joseph Haydn (HY-den) was a musical genius. But he lived in a time when musicians were dependent on wealthy patrons for their very survival. In the 18th century much of the wealth and power in Europe was under the control of a few enormously rich families. These royal houses, such as the Bourbons in France, the Hapsburgs in Austria and the Romanovs in Russia, formed great dynasties supported by smaller kingdoms. Everyone else—peasant farmers, craftsmen, tradesmen, artists, and minor nobility—depended on these powerful princes for their livelihood. This was called the feudal system.

Haydn worked within this system. He spent much of his adult life employed by the Esterházys, an immensely wealthy Hungarian family who owned estates near the Austrian border. The Esterházy princes were music lovers who recognized and valued Haydn's genius. Still, they treated him as a servant.

Haydn's contract with the Esterházys required him to present himself to the prince every day at noon to discuss musical plans for the day. The prince addressed his servants, Haydn included, in the third person. So he wouldn't ask, "What have you composed for this evening?" Instead he would say, "What has Herr Haydn composed for this evening?"

This method of address emphasized that Haydn was a member of the lower classes. He had to wear a uniform. He had to set an example for the other musicians by his good behavior. He had to resolve any problems that occurred among the musicians. He had to teach the singers and rehearse the orchestra. He had to take care of the musical instruments and the musical scores in the Esterházys' extensive music library. He couldn't even resign without securing the approval of the prince. And all of Haydn's musical compositions were the property of Prince Esterházy. No copies were to be made without the prince's permission.

But instead of feeling bitter about all the work that was expected of him, Haydn was cheerful. He told his first biographer, Georg Griesinger, who spent the last 10 years of Haydn's life as a close friend, "My Prince was content with all my works, I received approval. I could, as head of an orchestra, make experiments, observe what enhanced an effect, and what weakened it, thus improving, adding to, cutting away, and running risks. I was set apart from the world, there was nobody in my vicinity to confuse and annoy me in my course, and so I had to be original."

Haydn had a sunny disposition that thrived on hard work, and a kindly nature that made him respected and admired by the musicians he worked with. They responded to his gentle discipline by doing their best for him. They were willing to come to rehearsal whenever Haydn had an experiment he wanted to try out. So they called him "Papa" Haydn even though he had no children.

In return, Haydn would frequently write to the prince to ask for new instruments or other items the musicians needed. Other

This is the palace at Esterháza where Haydn was employed most of his life. He was appointed full Kapellmeister in 1766 and was the director of about 15-20 musicians at the court of Prince Nikolaus (Miklós) Esterházy. Prince Esterházy had two palaces known as Esterháza: one was in Eisenstadt; the second was built as a summer home in Fertod and modeled after Versailles.

times he asked the prince not to carry out a punishment for a mistake a musician had made.

Prince Nikolaus Esterházy once fired a tenor and a soprano in the choir who made plans to marry without first asking his permission. Haydn asked the prince to change his mind and allow the two singers to remain employed. Whatever Haydn said, it worked. Neither singer was forced to leave. Another time, an orchestra member accidentally burned down a house. He almost went to jail, but Haydn was able to reduce the punishment to being dismissed and the man was soon rehired.

The most famous incident where Haydn helped his musicians occurred in 1772.

Eight years previously, Prince Nikolaus Esterházy visited France and saw the royal palace at Versailles. Nikolaus returned and built his own lavish palace in Fertod, which was called Esterháza. It had more than 100 guest rooms. There was an art gallery filled with the finest paintings from Italy and Holland and a library with 75,000 books. There was an opera theater with seating for 400 and a smaller marionette theater. The elaborate gardens were described in the guidebook to Esterháza, which Nikolaus wrote himself: "Art and nature are here combined in a noble and magnificent manner. In every corner there is something to catch the eye: statues, temples, grottoes and fountains."

When Haydn was not at Esterházy Palace, this was his home in Eisenstadt. This is a watercolor painting of the courtyard.

But the real fame of Esterháza rested on the music of Joseph Haydn. He composed symphonies, operas and chamber music such as quartets and trios to show off the talents of his musicians.

Originally Esterháza had been planned as a summer home. The Esterházys still spent most of the year at their home castle in Eisenstadt. But as the gardens and theaters, the performances and entertainments became more lavish, Nikolaus began staying longer and longer. And where Nikolaus stayed, his musicians had to stay.

This was a hardship for the musicians because their families couldn't live at Esterháza. There was no room for them. Things came to a head in 1772 as "summer" stretched on and on with no end in sight. The musicians begged Haydn to ask Prince Nikolaus to allow them to return home to Eisenstadt.

Haydn was wary of confronting Nikolaus with a direct request. It would be too easy for the prince to say "No." So he thought of a better approach. He wrote a new symphony to be performed for the prince and his court. But it would have a twist.

Nearly every symphony in Haydn's day had four movements, with the final movement played at a fast, cheerful tempo. The new symphony's final movement began in the usual upbeat fashion. But after about three minutes, there was a pause. Then the musicians began playing at a much slower tempo. Nikolaus must have been confused. And his bafflement would have increased about a minute later when two musicians suddenly stopped playing, gathered up their music, blew out their candles, then stood up and walked off the stage. One by one, the other players did the same. Soon there were just two violinists left. They played a brief, haunting duet. Then they too snuffed out their candles and departed. The prince and his audience were left facing a dark and empty stage.

This is the story behind Haydn's Farewell Symphony. It was not only a brilliant piece of music but also a charming message to the prince. It expressed the sadness and longing that the musicians felt for their families. Nikolaus got the hint. He quickly granted the musicians their vacation.

Entertainment at the Esterháza Palace was quite lavish. When a new opera house was built at the palace, Haydn wrote operas. From the mid-1770s, regular performances were given. In 1779 the opera house burnt down, but it was rebuilt and it re-opened in 1781. Although his operas never gained wide exposure, much of Haydn's music was eventually published in all the main European centers under a revised contract with the Esterházys.

FYInfo

VERSAILLES

The French Royal Palace at Versailles (ver-SIGH) started in 1623 as a small hunting lodge built by King Louis XIII outside of Paris. King Louis XIII liked it so much he had it made larger in 1631. His son, who succeeded his father as King Louis XIV in 1643 at the age of five and eventually became known as the Sun King, liked the chateau too. But he thought it was too small. Starting in 1661, he had his architects design a much larger chateau completely surrounding the original building.

Magnificent official state apartments glorified the Sun King. The terrace of the central building was transformed into the magnificent Hall of Mirrors, which is almost as long as a football field. It symbolized the absolute power of Louis XIV. North and South wings were added. Two large curved buildings called the Stables were constructed in the front court to provide shelter for the king's 600 fine horses. The court musicians and other servants also lived there.

In 1682, Versailles replaced Paris as the official residence of the king. And he kept adding to what was already there. By the end of his reign in 1715, the complex had grown to include 235 acres of gardens, an enclosed park of 4,200 acres, and a hunting park of about 14,800 acres. The total area was 23 square miles, the size of many large cities today.

Louis XV continued the family tradition of building at Versailles. His most important construction in the main buildings was the opera house. It was completed in 1770 to celebrate the marriage of the Dauphin (who would become Louis XVI) to Marie Antoinette, the daughter of Empress Maria Theresa of Austria. He also built a smaller chateau, the Petit (small) Trianon. Louis XVI gave it to Marie Antoinette when he became king in 1774. She was responsible for creating the Hamlet, a replica of a peasant village on the outside but decorated with marble and royal furnishings inside the rooms.

But its splendor—the architecture, gardens, fountains, magnificent furnishings and decorations, statues and paintings—placed a crushing burden of taxes on the French people during the 18th century. That was a major cause of the French Revolution, which began in 1789 and ended Versailles' era as the official royal residence. Now it has been restored as a museum and is one of the favorite tourist attractions in France.

The house in Rohrau where Haydn was born painted by artist Johann Reinhart. Rohrau is a small village in Austria near the border with Hungary. The house is maintained as a museum today and visitors can see the small pianoforte Haydn is supposed to have played, as well as letters and other memorabilia.

CHAPTER

2

A Working Childhood

F ranz Joseph Haydn was born on April 1, 1732, or at least
that was the date his father recorded in his Hausbuch
(house book). Joseph—he always referred to himself by his
middle name—told another of his biographers, Albert Christoph
Dies, that his younger brother Michael insisted that the actual date
had been March 31st "because he doesn't want it said that I came
into the world as an April fool." Joseph's father, Mathias, was a
wheelwright in the little town of Rohrau in lower Austria near the
Hungarian border. His mother was Anna Maria Haydn, who had
been a cook before her marriage. They had twelve children, of
whom six survived past infancy. Joseph, whose nickname was
Sepperl, was the second child and the first son.

Mathias Haydn had a beautiful tenor voice and loved to sing.
In the evenings Mathias would take out his harp, which he played
by ear, and sing Austrian folksongs. Little Sepperl joined in the
singing. He also pretended to play a violin by using a stick as an
imaginary bow across his arm. He had seen the local schoolmaster
play the violin and wanted to learn how.

When Sepperl was six years old, a relative from his father's
birthplace of Hainburg came to visit. Johann Franck was a school-

master and responsible for the music at the local church. When Franck heard Sepperl's beautiful singing voice, he spoke to Mathias and Maria about taking the boy with him to Hainburg. It was a difficult decision, but Sepperl's parents wanted a better life for the boy. A musical education would open the door to many opportunities.

At the age when boys now would be entering first grade, young Joseph went to Hainburg. He and the others in the schoolmaster's care had lessons from 7:00 to 10:00 in the morning. Then they sang at Mass in the church. In the afternoon there was schoolwork until 3:00, and in the evening they had lessons in playing the violin and the clavier (an early form of the piano). The boy's musical ability was obvious. He took part in all of the musical events in Hainburg.

His life was not easy. Franck's wife did not keep the boys' clothing clean and mended as Joseph's mother had done. Franck was overworked and frequently disciplined the boys severely. They were not well fed. But all the difficulties did not dampen Joseph's naturally sunny disposition. He had his music. He had a real violin to play. Late in his life he praised Franck to Griesinger: "I shall owe it to that man even in my grave that he taught me so many things, though in the process I received more thrashings than food."

After Joseph had studied with Franck for two years, Georg Reutter, the choirmaster of St. Stephen's Cathedral in Vienna, came to Hainburg looking for boys to sing in his choir. Reutter was impressed with Joseph's singing. He engaged the eight-year-old as a chorister.

Once again the boy found himself sustained by the music he loved while enduring a difficult life. The boys in the cathedral choir had religious instruction and lessons in Latin, mathematics, and writing as well as instruction in singing, violin, and clavier. The purpose of their music lessons was to improve their performance in the choir. They had no lessons in music theory or composition. In these areas Haydn was left to educate himself by listening carefully to the music that most impressed him. And there was plenty.

When Haydn was eight years old, he joined the choir at St. Stephen's Cathedral in Vienna, shown here in this tinted lithograph.

Haydn later told a biographer, "I heard the finest music in all forms that was to be heard in my time, and of that there was much in Vienna." Reutter encouraged the young Haydn to create variations on the music he had to sing in church. This soon led the boy to develop ideas of his own.

Life in the cathedral was hard. The discipline was harsh and the food was limited. The choirmaster was allowed only a

Western Europe

Austria

Slovakia

Hungary

Vienna
Hainburg
Eisenstadt
Sopron
Bratislava
Fertőd

This map shows how Austria, Hungary, and Slovakia look today. But during the 18th century, there were royal families who were very wealthy and powerful. Those, like the Esterházy princes, who were allied with the Hapsburg dynasty, had widespread properties. There were no "national" boundaries as we understand them today. Instead, there were shifting alliances of the great royal families, and as the alliances shifted, so did the boundaries of their countries. Eisenstadt was to the east of the Hungarian border in the 1700s and was a part of Hungary during that time. Vienna was, and still is in Austria. One of the original Esterházy homes is in Eisenstadt, but the big palace that Prince Nikolaus modeled after Versailles was built in Fertod, just east of Sopron, in Hungary.

small amount of money to pay for the boys' food. The boys looked forward anxiously to the concerts outside of the cathedral. Wealthy families who had them sing for special occasions provided meals. These events were the only times the boys had enough to eat.

They worked hard. In the cathedral they sang Mass every morning and Vespers every afternoon. For feast days and special occasions the music would be very elaborate. They needed extra

Empress MariaTheresa was part of the Royal Hapsburg (Habsburg) family, one of Europe's most famous royal families. She built Schönbrunn Palace in Vienna. This is a painting of her and her sons by J. L. Maurice.

rehearsals. The boys also sang at marriages and funerals and for private concerts and public ceremonies.

Under the pressure of such a hard schedule, it's small wonder that the boys were not always under control on their outings. When they went to sing for the Hapsburg Empress Maria Theresa at her new palace in Vienna, the scaffolding around the building had not yet been removed. With whoops of joy the boys began climbing it. The Empress was furious at the noise they made. She came to the window and threatened to have them beaten if they climbed the scaffolding again. The next day Joseph climbed to the top to impress his friends. It certainly impressed the Empress, who was furious at his disobedience and demanded that he be thrashed. The choirmaster was only too glad to obey.

Things got worse. When Joseph was 17, his voice began to change. He was no longer able to sing the high notes, which made him almost useless in the choir. His younger brother Michael had joined the choir a few years after Joseph. Michael had a beautiful soprano voice and was now the darling of the audiences. At one performance the Empress was so impressed she gave Michael 24 golden coins. Then she added that Joseph "sang like a crow."

A little later Joseph went too far with one of his jokes. He cut off the pigtail of the boy sitting in front of him in the choir. The choirmaster called Joseph to his office and said he was to be whipped. Joseph told the choirmaster that he would leave rather than be beaten, but Reutter beat the boy anyway. Then he put Joseph out on the streets of Vienna.

It was a cold November day. Joseph Haydn was homeless and penniless. He owned only the clothes he was wearing plus two other worn shirts. ◆

VIENNA FYInfo

The royal Hapsburg family ruled a huge empire from their imperial capital, Vienna. This beautiful city is on the Danube River near the border between Austria and Hungary. After the defeat of a Turkish army near Vienna in 1683, the city soon attracted the intellectual and artistic elite of central Europe. By the beginning of the 18th century it was a cultural center for art, architecture, theater, literature, and above all, music. A brilliant court surrounded the Hapsburgs. In spite of their domination of the city, however, the nobility made up only a small minority of the population.

Below the powerful princes whose estates surrounded Vienna were members of the upper middle class. These were bankers, merchants, wealthy politicians and successful lawyers. A large part of the middle class population consisted of master craftsmen, shopkeepers, and tradesmen. Most of the industry in Vienna was in small workshops. Each craft—carriage making, tailoring, grinding grain, producing ceramics, iron working and dozens of others—had its own guild. In these guilds, apprentices learned the skills to become journeymen. The journeymen in turn learned to become master craftsmen.

Below them were the members of the lower class. These were unskilled workers and the servants who cooked and cleaned in the houses of the middle and upper class citizens and the palaces of the nobility. They cared for animals, drove carriages, and delivered goods.

Members of the nobility kept orchestras to entertain their guests. Many had their own theaters where operas and plays were performed. These rich noblemen competed with each other to have the best composers and the best singers. The churches also employed musicians. They kept choirs to sing the music of the Mass and other services.

As the 18th century progressed, social problems in Vienna and other European cities increased. The lavish spending and the elaborate entertainments of the nobility increased. At the same time poverty increased.

As a result, Vienna in the 18th century was a city of dramatic contrasts. It was a beautiful city, known throughout Europe for its magnificent palaces and cathedrals. Vienna's music was the finest in the world. But the brilliant and lavish lives of the few were supported by the hard work and desperate poverty of the many.

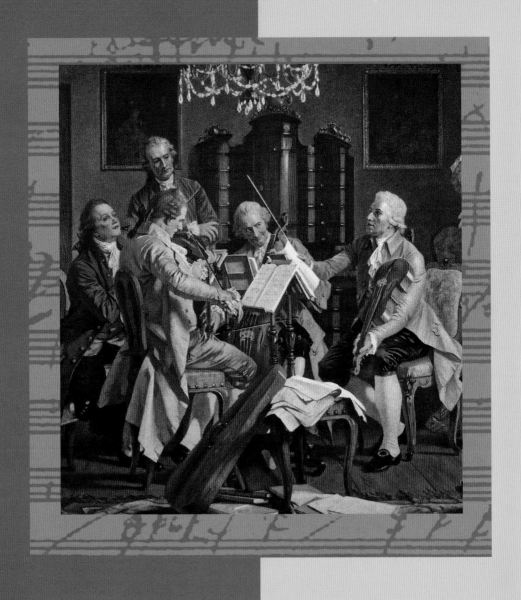

Haydn is often given credit for being the father of the string quartet. Mozart frequently confessed it was from Haydn that he learned how to compose for four stringed instruments. It was one of Haydn's most successful mediums for his artistic expression.

CHAPTER
3

Success Begins

But despite his sudden ill fortunate, Haydn did have a cheerful nature that attracted friends. As he walked the streets of Vienna, he met Michael Spangler, an acquaintance who had also been at St. Stephens. Spangler was scarcely in a better financial situation than Joseph. He lived in a little attic room with his wife and infant son. Nonetheless, when he heard of the boy's troubles he insisted that Joseph come home with him.

Joseph was grateful, and stayed with the little family for a few months. Then another baby arrived and the Spanglers needed more space. Joseph knew that he would have to find another place to live. Years later he would have a chance to repay the Spanglers' kindness: the new baby, a little girl, grew up to be the soprano whose job he saved after she married without Prince Esterhazy's permission.

Soon another great kindness helped the boy. Johann William Buchholz, a friend of his father, heard of Joseph's difficulties and lent him enough money to rent his own little attic room, with a leaky roof and no stove. He bought an old harpsichord to practice and compose on. Almost immediately his fortunes began to improve.

Joseph found a few students who paid a small amount for music lessons. He sang tenor in a cathedral choir. He played the violin for services at a monastery and frequently for parties or serenades in the evenings. And when he was not working, he was at his harpsichord composing. He wrote music for his keyboard students to play, simple sonatas that he could tailor to their level of ability. He wrote trios to play in serenades and dance music for parties.

He was poor but happy. "When I was sitting at my old worm-eaten clavier, I envied no king his lot," he later wrote.

Since Haydn had no formal training in composition, he studied whatever music he could find. At about this time he came upon the first six keyboard sonatas of Carl Philipp Emanuel Bach, the son of the famous Johann Sebastian Bach. Haydn told Griesinger, "I did not come away from my keyboard until I had played through them, and whoever knows me thoroughly must realize that I owe a great deal to Emanuel Bach, and that I understood him and studied him diligently."

One unusual aspect of housing in 18th century Vienna was that people of different social classes would live in the same building. The first floor contained luxurious apartments occupied by the nobility. Just above those would be the residences of wealthy tradesmen or artists. And on the upper floors were the little rooms of the poor, such as the young Haydn. Joseph could hardly have hoped for better housemates than he found in his building. On the first floor lived Princess Esterházy, the mother of the princes that Haydn would eventually work for. The famous poet Pietro Metastasio and his friends the Martinez family were on the third floor.

The eldest daughter of this family, Mariana Martinez, was a gifted young lady. Metastasio arranged for Joseph to give Mariana lessons in singing and keyboard playing. He also introduced Haydn to an Italian composer, Nicola Porpora. The composer was old and crabby, but he hired Haydn as his accompanist. Joseph was used to harsh treatment in exchange for education, so he didn't mind the old man's curses. He was finally learning from a professional composer. Haydn later said in an autobiographical letter, "I wrote diligently, but not quite soundly, until at last I had the privilege of learning the true fundamentals of composition from the celebrated Herr Porpora."

Haydn's great natural ability was finally receiving the benefit of formal instruction in composing and music theory from a mas-

One aspect of 18th century Vienna during the feudal system was that different classes of people would live in the same building. The first floor contained luxurious apartments of the nobility. Just above them would be the wealthy tradesmen. On the upper floors were the little rooms of the poor such as the young Joseph Haydn or the peasants shown making music in the painting on the left. The famous Italian composer Nicola Porpora is pictured on the right.

ter. Sometimes his compositions, such as his first quartets, would be played at musical gatherings. His professional reputation was increasing, and eventually he more than doubled the rates that he was charging for music lessons. Also, as he worked for Porpora he met other celebrated musicians and the wealthy amateurs who were music lovers and patrons.

It was just such a music-loving nobleman who recommended Haydn to Count Karl von Morzin of Bohemia. The Count hired Joseph as his Kapellmeister, or music director, most likely in 1759. In addition to his salary, he received all of his meals, housing, travel expenses, and uniforms. It was the first real security Haydn had ever known. Count Morzin had an orchestra of 16 musicians. They traveled with him to his estate in Bohemia in the summer and played in Vienna during the winter. Haydn had to organize the music, rehearse, and perform with the orchestra. He composed his first symphony for this orchestra.

Haydn's position with Count Morzin didn't last very long. The Count got into financial difficulties and was forced to disband his orchestra. Prince Anton Esterházy, a cultured and educated amateur musician and the head of the most important Hungarian noble family, heard that Haydn was available. The Esterházy Kapellmeister, Gregor Werner, was getting old. Werner was a good composer, but he had worked for the prince at his palace at Eisenstadt for 30 years. The job was now too much for him. Prince Anton offered Joseph Haydn the position of Vice-Kapellmeister in 1761. Werner would continue to compose and conduct the church music. All of the other music would be Haydn's responsibility.

THE SYMPHONY

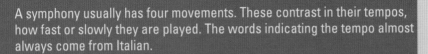

The word "symphony" is a Greek word that means "sounding together." Sometimes we use the word to mean an orchestra in which all the different instruments play together. More often we use it to mean a particular musical form that was developed during the Classical Period in the late 18th century. It was a time when balance, order, and form were preferred over the expression of emotion.

A symphony usually has four movements. These contrast in their tempos, how fast or slowly they are played. The words indicating the tempo almost always come from Italian.

The first movement is generally in a rapid tempo such as allegro, an Italian word meaning "fast." The second movement contrasts with the first by being played at a slower tempo such as andante or adagio, which means "slow" or "slower." The third movement is again in a rapid tempo. The fourth usually is also rapid; it frequently has the fastest tempo of all.

The internal structures of the four movements are quite different. The first movement is usually the longest and most serious. It typically uses sonata form, the structure used in much of classical music. Sonata form has three sections. The first section is called the exposition because it introduces two (occasionally more) musical themes, or motifs. These usually contrast with each other—one might be quite loud and dramatic, while the other could be soft and lyrical. The second section is the development. In this section the composer takes the original themes and changes them in a number of ways. Third is the recapitulation, largely a repeat of the exposition. Sometimes the movement ends with a short closing passage, or coda.

The fourth movement of a symphony is the least predictable. Usually the tempo is rapid and the themes upbeat so the listeners come away happy. It might restate the motifs from the first movement, or it might introduce entirely new themes. Many times it is in the form of a rondo. A rondo has one main theme, which alternates with several different themes.

The theater at Esterháza opened in 1768. (The theater in this painting is at Versailles, where Prince Esterházy first became interested in building a palace of his own.) The first performance was Haydn's comic opera The Apothecary. During the 1770s the prince became more and more interested in operas.

Musician

While Joseph Haydn was living in Vienna, he had fallen in love with one of his students, Therese Keller. But her parents ordered her to become a nun. In a rebound marriage, Haydn married Therese's older sister, Maria Anna, in 1760. His marriage was unhappy. Of all the difficult people that Haydn had to deal with in his life, about the only one that he didn't get along with was his wife. She was mean, had no interest in music, and could not have children. She even used sheets of her husband's music to line her pastry tins. Eventually they separated, but Haydn refused to consider a divorce. He supported her financially until she died in 1802.

Maybe it was because his marriage was so unhappy that Haydn put all his energy into his music. In addition, the Esterházys eventually spent nearly all their time at Esterháza in Fertod and Haydn followed them. Its remote location meant that he became very isolated from the cultural scene in Vienna. He became one of the most productive composers who ever lived.

After only one year, Prince Anton Esterházy died and his brother, Prince Nikolaus, succeeded him, giving Haydn a substantial raise. Haydn would serve Nikolaus for nearly 30 years. But things were difficult at first because Kapellmeister Werner resented the young Haydn. The older man complained that Haydn was lazy and neglected his duties. Nikolaus wrote Haydn a letter ordering him to change his ways. The Prince particularly told Haydn to produce more compositions. In particular, Nikolaus wanted music for the baryton, a kind of cello that he played himself.

One result of the Prince's order was that Haydn began keeping a list of all the works he had composed. He added to the list as he composed more music. The quantity of works on the list is nearly as amazing as its quality! The list includes 160 works for Nikolaus to play on the baryton. In his first six years with the Esterházys, Haydn wrote more than 30 symphonies. He also wrote many concertos for his outstanding soloists, such as the famous violinist Alois Luigi Tomasini. Henceforth, Joseph Haydn was never accused of laziness.

After Werner died in 1766, Haydn became responsible for composing the church music. This was in addition to composing symphonies, operas, the baryton compositions and such classical favorites as trios, string quartets, and piano sonatas.

The theater at Esterháza opened in 1768. The first performance was Haydn's comic opera *The Apothecary*. During the 1770s the prince became more and more interested in operas. Many of them were presented for special occasions like the marriage of his niece in 1770. In 1773 the Empress Maria Theresa was a guest at a performance of one of Haydn's operas. At the end she commented, "When I want to hear a good opera, I go to Esterháza." Haydn was presented to the empress and received her praise. Did she remember that he was the choirboy she had beaten for climbing the scaffolding at her palace?

From 1776 to 1790, Haydn added the role of opera director to his other duties. The Prince's love of opera increased and eventually the season occupied ten months of the year. By 1786, for example, eight new operas were presented along with nine revivals for about 125 separate performances. All of these, including rehearsals, were under Haydn's direction.

To produce an opera, Haydn had to either compose the work himself or to find other appropriate music. If he composed the music himself, he first had to find a suitable libretto (the words in which the story is told). If he chose an opera by another composer, he frequently made large revisions, substituting his own arias for any he didn't like. He had to supervise the copying of the parts, coach the singers, and rehearse the orchestra and singers. He produced operas for the marionette theater as well.

It seems hard to believe that Haydn continued to compose other music. But he did. In addition to the operas and church music, he had to rehearse and perform two concerts every week. For these he continued to write symphonies and concertos. At the same time, he returned to writing string quartets.

In 1779, Prince Nikolaus drew up a new contract. It allowed Haydn to write music for others. Of course his heavy demands for music to be performed at Esterháza made it difficult. But for a composer with as many ideas as Haydn, it was possible.

For a while Haydn's main source of outside income was from selling copies of his music to monasteries and members of the nobility. Then he began selling directly to publishers. At times he had difficulty keeping up with the ever-increasing demand for his compositions.

As his music gained more and more recognition, Haydn found it increasingly difficult to spend all of his time in isolation at Esterháza. He longed for the cultural life of Vienna. Eventually he was given leave to spend a month or two there each winter.

It was probably during one of these visits in the early 1780s that he met Wolfgang Amadeus Mozart. The two became good friends and admirers of each other's work. These two creative geniuses understood and respected each other. There was no competition or jealousy between them.

Haydn had another close friend in Vienna, Maria Anna von Genzinger. The wife of one of Prince Nikolaus's doctors, she was an intelligent and cultured noblewoman who admired Haydn's music. He wrote many letters to Frau Genzinger during his long periods away from Vienna. From these letters we learn how isolated Haydn felt at Esterháza.

In September of 1790, Prince Nikolaus died. His son Prince Anton had no interest in music. He disbanded the orchestra. Joseph Haydn remained officially as Kapellmeister but had no duties. He was free to go where he wished and do what he wanted to. Of course he headed for Vienna.

STORM AND STRESS

Johann Wolfgang von Goethe (GER-tah) influenced the art of 18th and 19th century Europe more than any other person. His writing filled nearly 150 volumes. Half of these were literary works such as poetry, novels, and plays. The rest was scientific writing, private diaries and letters.

The subject of Goethe's writing was his experiences, his own life. His works of fiction, poetry and drama are closely drawn from actual events. The characters are based on his friends and the women he fell in love with—and he fell in love frequently. Even his scientific writings are personal in that he wrote from his own observations.

Goethe was born in Frankfurt in present-day Germany on August 28, 1749. His grandfather was an official of the city; his father was a wealthy man who had the boy educated by tutors. Although it was apparent by the time he was ten years old that the boy was a born poet, his father sent him to study law at Leipzig. He did study law, but he also wrote poetry and fell in love. Before finishing his studies, however, he became very ill and returned to Frankfurt.

Two years later, in 1770, his health had recovered. After a bitter quarrel with his father, he went off to Strasbourg to finish his legal studies. He did complete his study of law, but much more important was the circle of friends he met there. He attracted a group of young men who were strongly influenced by the works of Rousseau, Shakespeare and the ancient Greeks. They began a literary movement they called Sturm und Drang ("storm and stress"). They insisted upon a return to nature, the importance of strong emotion, and the cult of genius.

In 1774 he published *The Sorrows of Young Werther*. It was a tale of a sensitive young man who suffers the torments of unrequited love and eventually commits suicide. Except for the suicide, it was an accurate record of Goethe's experiences. Soon he was famous.

His new life came in the form of an invitation from Duke Karl Augustus of Weimar. The Duke admired *Werther* and invited Goethe to visit his court. Goethe soon became the Duke's close friend and eventually the administrator of his lands. Weimar became his home for the rest of his life.

He completed the long play *Faust*, which he began in 1773, just before his death in 1832. It tells the story of a man who sells his soul to the Devil but is redeemed by love for other people. It is his most famous work.

Haydn remained productive nearly to the end of his life. He became Vienna's grand old man of music: an inspiration to younger generations. This painting of Haydn was done by Thomas Hardy.

CHAPTER 5

Fame

Haydn was free at last. He still had the title of Kapellmeister and the salary that went with it. But he had no duties. He planned to settle in Vienna and enjoy the rich cultural life he had so longed for while he was isolated at Esterháza. He did experience such a life, but not in Vienna.

One day a man appeared at Haydn's door. According to Haydn's biographer Dies, he announced, "I am Salomon from London and have come to fetch you. Tomorrow we shall conclude an agreement."

That is exactly what they did. For a large amount of money, Haydn was to compose, direct and perform six symphonies, an opera and 20 other pieces in London.

Some of Haydn's friends told him that he was too old for such a strenuous journey. Others said that the political situation was dangerous because of the revolution in France that was threatening the stability of all of Europe.

Mozart tried to convince him not to go, saying, "You don't know the language."

Haydn replied, "My language is understood all over the world." He meant that anyone could understand his music.

Both friends cried when they parted. Mozart said, "We shall not see each other ever again."

He was right. Mozart died the following year at the age of 35 while Haydn was in London.

"My arrival caused a great sensation throughout the whole city," he wrote to Maria Anna Genzinger. "If I wanted, I could dine out every day."

The concerts that Salomon arranged were a great success. Haydn was a guest of the Prince of Wales, heir to the throne of England. He received the title of Doctor of Music from Oxford University.

Joseph Haydn had spent his life being treated as a servant, wearing a uniform and following orders. Now he was the honored guest of English royalty and nobility. He wrote to Frau von Genzinger, "Oh, my dear good lady, how sweet is some degree of freedom. I had a good employer, but I was sometimes forced to depend on base persons. I often sighed for release, and now I have it."

He made many friends in England. One was an educated widow who took piano lessons from Haydn and fell in love with him. He later told Dies, "She was a very attractive woman. Had I been free I should certainly have married her."

Haydn composed some of his greatest symphonies and string quartets while he was in England. One of them, Symphony No. 96, is nicknamed the "Miracle Symphony." As soon as its first performance had been completed, many of the audience members rushed

Haydn made two visits to London. The first tour was from 1791 to 1792 and the second tour was in 1794-1795. It was during the second tour that Haydn produced the oratorio The Creation. Haydn was influenced by the oratorios he had heard in London by George Frideric Handel. This painting depicts his crossing the English Channel in a storm where he is contemplating writing The Creation.

toward the stage to applaud Haydn. Suddenly a huge chandelier came crashing down—right on the spot where those people had been just moments before. Everyone considered it a miracle that no one was killed or even hurt.

In June of 1792, Haydn's first trip to England ended and he returned to Vienna. On his way back he stopped in Bonn. There he met a young man who wanted to be a composer. His name was Ludwig van Beethoven. Haydn was impressed and agreed to accept the 22-year-old as a student when he came to Vienna.

Young Beethoven had been invited to study with Haydn. On his way back to Vienna after returning from a tour in London, Haydn stopped briefly in Bonn. There he saw music composed by Beethoven and said he would accept Beethoven as a student if he came to Vienna. As it turned out, Beethoven was not grateful.

Haydn's return to Vienna was quiet. After the fuss that had been made over him in London, the lack of interest in his home city must have been disappointing.

Soon he received another shock. Maria Anna von Genzinger died suddenly at the age of 43. And to make matters even worse, he didn't work well with Beethoven. In spite of his youth and inexperience, Beethoven was arrogant and stubborn. The young Ludwig refused to take criticism. He was convinced that his teacher criticized his compositions because he was jealous.

In January of 1794, Haydn again departed for England. His second visit was even more successful than the first. The symphonies he composed and performed were among his best, and were received with great praise. King George III, a music lover, asked Haydn to live permanently in London, and Queen Charlotte offered him a suite in Windsor Castle if he would stay.

It was a tempting offer, but Haydn was tired. The constant round of social events was exciting, but difficult for a man in his 60s. Furthermore, Prince Anton had just died, and his son Nikolaus II wrote to Haydn to say that he was going to reinstate the orchestra. Haydn was asked to return as Kapellmeister once again.

In an age when there was no social security, he did not feel he could refuse to return to duty with the Esterházys, especially since Nikolaus had largely abandoned Esterháza. That meant that Haydn could live in Vienna for most of the year, with summers in Eisenstadt. The one duty Prince Nikolaus required was that Haydn compose a Mass for the name-day of the prince's wife each year. He produced six that are among his greatest compositions.

While in England, Haydn had been inspired by Handel's oratorios. Before he left England, Haydn had been given a copy of a text based on John Milton's long poem *Paradise Lost.* Translated into German, it became the basis of Haydn's magnificent oratorio *The Creation*, which premiered in 1798. Encouraged by that success, he began another oratorio, *The Seasons.* The work went slowly because his health was failing. It was his last major work and was performed in May of 1801.

This engraving is of the town square in Eisenstadt, which today, is a part of Austria. Eisenstadt is the home of Franz Joseph Haydn. It is also where the Esterházys had one of their palaces. Haydn went to work for Prince Esterházy first in Eisenstadt, which back then, was a part of Hungary. Then, the Prince built a new, more elaborate palace as a summer home, and spent most of the year there. The new palace was built near Fertod, on the Austria-Hungary border. It is situated in Hungary today.

Although he no longer had the strength to compose, Haydn received honors and visitors from all over the world. His two first biographers, Dies and Griesinger, came whenever he had the strength to speak with them. He told them many stories about his life and work. When the French army occupied Vienna in 1809, Haydn was near death. Even so, he asked his servants to carry him to the piano so he could play the Austrian national anthem, which he had composed more than 10 years earlier.

Joseph Haydn died peacefully in his sleep on May 31, 1809 at the age of 77.

He had a quiet funeral and burial in Vienna. But it would be nearly 150 years before he would rest in peace.

In 1820, the current Prince Esterházy exhumed the composer's body for reburial at the family estate in Eisenstadt. When he opened the coffin, he was horrified to find a headless Haydn!

Two young students of phrenology—the "science" of studying personality by examining the contours of the skull—had bribed the gravedigger soon after his burial in Vienna to open the coffin. They had taken Haydn's head and enclosed it an ornate black wooden box with a silk lining.

When Prince Esterházy discovered their identity, he sent police to get the skull back. But they couldn't find it. More than 75 years later, the surviving thief willed it to a museum in Vienna that had a number of Haydn's personal effects. The museum hung on to it for another 60 years. By then, the Esterházys had constructed an elaborate memorial to the composer in Eisenstadt's church and the museum let them have the skull in 1954. Haydn had become whole again.

Because he had a good sense of humor and enjoyed practical jokes, Haydn might have forgiven the prank. He once wrote, "Since God has given me a cheerful heart, He will forgive me for serving him cheerfully."

He had spent most of his life serving aristocratic princes, and lived to see the dawning of a new age, a new kind of society in which men were more equal. His music proves that true magnificence comes not from wealth and power, but from the creativity of human genius.

Haydn's skull rested in a museum in Vienna for nearly 60 years. In 1954, Haydn got his head back to be buried with the rest of him in Eisenstadt.

FYInfo

THE FRENCH REVOLUTION

The French Revolution was the single most important influence on the intellectual and political life in Europe at the end of the 18th century. Before the revolution nearly everyone in France was unhappy. The nobility wanted the power that the king had taken away from them. The middle class was unhappy because of the privileges the nobility had. Both the peasants and the middle class hated the tax system. They had to pay heavy taxes but the aristocrats, who had most of the wealth, didn't have to.

The nation was bankrupt because of extravagant spending on magnificent palaces like Versailles and ambitious wars. The French had lost most of their colonies to Britain. To get revenge on the British, the French became involved in helping the American colonists in the Revolutionary War.

On July 14, 1789, 13 years after the American Declaration of Independence, the common people of Paris stormed the Bastille. This huge prison was a symbol of oppression. After the fall of the Bastille, the peasants rose up all over France. Their slogan was "Liberty, Equality, Fraternity." Many members of the nobility fled to Austria or England for their safety.

In August the newly formed French National Assembly abolished the feudal system and adopted a "Declaration of the Rights of Man and of the Citizen." Women invaded the palace, intending to kill Marie Antoinette, but she hid in the king's chambers. The mob forced the royal family to return to Paris where they virtually became prisoners.

During 1790 the National Assembly and the king tried to establish a constitutional monarchy, but the attempts failed. The king was secretly trying to get foreign powers to help him end the revolution. In June 1791 the royal family tried to escape to Austria, but they were captured and returned to Paris.The monarchy fell the following year and the royal family was imprisoned.

In January, 1793 Louis XVI was beheaded by a guillotine. Marie Antoinette suffered the same fate in August. The guillotine became the symbol of the Reign of Terror that followed. Not only members of the nobility but also leaders of the revolution who turned against each other had their heads cut off. Not until the rise of Napoleon Bonaparte in 1799 did the French find a leader strong enough to restore order and defeat France's foreign enemies.

Selected Works

Orchestral Music
108 symphonies, especially Symphony No. 45, ("Farewell"), Symphony No. 88, Symphony No. 94 ("Surprise"), Symphony No. 96 ("Miracle"), Symphony No. 100 ("Military"), Symphony No. 101 ("Clock"), Symphony No. 103 ("Drumroll") and Symphony No. 104 ("London")
31 concertos, especially two for cello and orchestra and one for harpsichord and orchestra
16 overtures

Chamber Music
77 string quartets; 18 favorites are six each in Op. 20, Op. 33, and Op. 76.
21 string trios
46 piano trios

Operas
17 operas, including *Orfeo ed Euridice*; 12 marionette operas and singspieles

Choral Music
The Creation oratorio
The Seasons oratorio
The Emperor's Hymn (Austrian national anthem)
14 masses, especially the *Lord Nelson Mass* and *Mass in Time of War*

Church Works
35 cantatas, choruses, and arias with orchestra

Miscellaneous Music
149 dance
398 folk-song arrangements
32 pieces for musical clock

Complete Works
A complete listing of the works of Franz Joseph Haydn can be found at many reliable Web sites on the internet. One interesting site is: www.classicalarchives.com/haydn.html. You can also download and listen to some of Haydn's music from this site.

Chronology

1732 born on March 31 or April 1
1738 goes to Hainburg with choirmaster and schoolmaster Johann Franck
1740 recruited for St. Stephen's Cathedral choir in Vienna by choirmaster Georg Reutter
1745 beaten for climbing the scaffolding at the Empress Maria Theresa's palace
1749 dismissed from cathedral choir for cutting off another chorister's pigtail
1753 first opera, *Der kumme Teufel*, performed in Vienna
1759 hired as Kapellmeister by Count Karl von Morzin and composed first symphony
1760 marries Maria Anna Keller
1761 hired as Vice-Kapellmeister by Prince Anton Esterházy
1762 Prince Anton dies; Prince Nikolaus Esterházy increases Haydn's salary
1766 becomes Kapellmeister
1776 first full-scale opera season at Esterháza
1790 Prince Nikolaus Esterházy dies; his son Anton dismisses the orchestra
1791 travels to London with Johann Peter Salomon for a concert series
1792 returns to Vienna; accepts Beethoven as a student
1794 second London concert series begins
1798 oratorio *The Creation* performed to great acclaim
1809 dies at home in Vienna on May 31

Timeline in History

1732 birth of George Washington
1750 Johann Sebastian Bach dies
1752 Benjamin Franklin invents lightning conductor
1755 Lisbon earthquake
1756 Seven Years' War between France and England begins (known as French and Indian War in American colonies)
1759 George Frideric Handel dies
1761 George III becomes King of England
1771 Luigi Galvani produces current electricity
1776 American colonies declare independence from England
1780 Maria Theresa, Empress of Austria, dies
1781 astronomer William Herschel discovers the planet Uranus
1783 American Revolution ends with the Paris Peace Treaty
1789 fall of the Bastille in Paris begins the French Revolution
1793 French King Louis XVI and Queen Marie Antoinette beheaded
1799 George Washington dies
1804 Napoleon declared Emperor of France
1812 United States declares war on Britain
1815 Wellington defeats Napoleon at Waterloo
1820 King George III of England dies

For Further Reading

For Young Adults:

Celenza, Anna Harwell. *The Farewell Symphony*. Watertown, MA: Charlesbridge
    Publishing, 2000.
Landon, H.C. Robbins. *Haydn*. New York: Praeger Publishers, 1972.
Mirsky, Reba Paeff. *Haydn*. Chicago: Follett Publishing Co., 1963.
Rachlin, Ann. *Haydn (Famous Children Series),* New York: Barrons Juveniles, 1992.
Thompson, Wendy. *Joseph Haydn*. New York: Viking, 1991

Works Consulted:

Butterworth, Neil. *Haydn, His Life and Times*. Tunbridge Wells, Kent, England: Midas
    Books, 1977.
Downs, Philip G. *Classical Music: The Era of Haydn, Mozart, and Beethoven*. New York:
    W.W. Norton & Co., 1992.
Gotwals, Vernon. *Joseph Haydn, Eighteenth-Century Gentleman and Genius*. Madison:
    University of Wisconsin Press, 1963.
Jones, David W. *Haydn: His Life and Music.* Bloomington: Indiana University Press,
    1988.
Landon, H. C. Robbins. *Haydn: The Early Years.* London: Thames & Hudson, 1995.
_____. *Haydn at Esterháza.* London: Thames & Hudson, 1995.
_____. *Haydn in England.* London: Thames & Hudson, 1995.
_____. *Haydn: The Late Years.* London: Thames & Hudson, 1995.
_____, ed. *The Collected Correspondence and London Notebooks of Joseph Haydn.*
    London: Thames & Hudson, 1959.
Larsen, Jens Peter. *The New Grove Haydn*. New York: W.W. Norton & Company,
    1982.
Sisman, Elaine. *Haydn and His World.* Princeton: Princeton University Press, 1997.
Wenborn. Neil. *Joseph Haydn: An Essential Guide to His Life and Works*. London:
    Pavilion Books Ltd., 1997.

On the Internet:

Biography of Franz Joseph Haydn
http://www.classicalarchives.com/bios/haydn_bio.html

Dallas Symphony Orchestra/Facts about Haydn
www.dsokids.com/2001/dso.asp?PageID=234

General Info about Haydn
http://w3.rz-berlin.mpg.de/cmp/haydnj.html

Biography of Haydn
www.composers.net/database/h/Haydn.html

Glossary

clavier – (KLAH-vee-er) a keyboard instrument with strings

adagio - (ih-DAJ-ee-oh) a slow tempo

allegro - (ih-LEG-row) quick or lively; a rapid tempo

andante - (ahn-DON-tay) moving or flowing; a medium tempo

chamber music - instrumental music for two, three, four or more instruments in which all parts have equal importance, such as a string quartet

classical music - music which emphasizes form and proportion rather than emotion

exhumed - (eggs-OOM-d) to dig up from a grave

feudal system - (FEW-dl SIS-tem) political organization based on the power of the royalty and nobility who owned the land and controlled the lives of farmers, servants and craftsmen

frau - (FROW) German form of "Mrs."

guillotine - (GIL-uh-teen) a machine for execution by beheading with a heavy blade

herr - (AIR) German form of "mister"

kapellmeister (kuh-PEL-MY-stur) - music director at an aristocratic court

marionette - (MAH-re-oh-NET) a puppet that is moved by strings fastened to its limbs and body

mass - a sequence of prayers and ceremonies used in the Catholic church; the music that is used during that time

minuet - (MIN-you-ETTE) a slow graceful dance; music in the rhythm of a minuet

motif - (moe-TEEF) a recurring element in a work of art

movement - shorter compositions which form the sections of a longer work such as a symphony, concerto, or sonata

oratorio - (or-uh-TOR-ee-oh) a long choral work, usually on a religious subject

quartet - (qwor-TET) a piece of music for four instruments, such as a string quartet for two violins, a viola, and a cello

romantic - art that emphasizes emotional expression

scherzo - (SKIRT-zoh) a sprightly and humorous musical composition

sonata - (suh-NOT-ah) an instrumental music composition typically of three or four contrasting movements

tempo - the speed at which a piece of music is played

trio - a piece of music for three instruments

vespers - a late afternoon or evening worship service; the music for this service

Index